KNOW ABOUT...

...NETS

Mary Gribbin & John Gri

What is a Planet?

A planet is a cold lump of rock and gas that moves around a star in an orbit. The Earth we live on is a planet. We can see other planets because they reflect light from the Sun. The Sun and its family of planets is called the Solar System.

When you look up at night and see a sky full of **stars**, some of the bright objects are actually planets.

What looks like a bright 'star' in this picture is actually the **planet** Venus. It is so bright that sometimes you can see it before the sky is dark.

Planets are closer to us than stars, and only shine because they reflect light from the **Sun**.

If you were to look at the stars every night, the stars will always be in the same place, whereas the planets will have moved. Stars do move, but we don't notice them moving because they are so far away.

The picture above is made up of lots of pictures of Venus. The pictures were taken several days apart to show how Venus moves across the sky.

The Solar System

Planets move across the sky because they are all going round the Sun in **orbits**.

This is a diagram of the **Solar System**. It shows our Sun with all the planets going around it. All the planets go round the Sun the same way, like runners going round a track.

The planets in the diagram are all in the right order so you can see which planets are nearest the Sun and which are the farthest away. In reality the planets are much more

spread out in the sky. One fun way to remember the order of the planets out from the Sun is with this sentence: **My Vicious Earthworm Might Just Swallow Us Now** (Mercury, Venus, Earth, Mars, Jupiter, Saturn, Uranus, Neptune).

The Sun is not a planet, it is a star. It is much bigger than any of the planets. Its surface is about 6000°C. It is so hot and bright that if you looked directly at it you would hurt your eyes very badly.

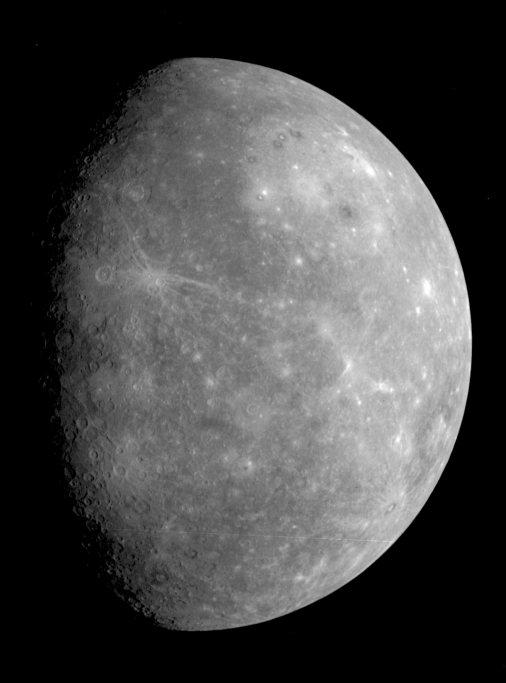

Mercury

Mercury is the closest planet to the Sun. It is smaller than Earth, and has a **diameter** of 4,880 km. It is bigger than the **Moon**, but like the Moon it doesn't have any air.

This picture was taken by a **spaceprobe** called Messenger in 2008. You can see in the photograph that there is no life on Mercury. It is a dead planet and looks very similar to the Moon. Its surface is covered by **craters** which are caused by lumps of rock smashing into its surface.

The word planet comes from a Greek word meaning wanderer. The name was chosen because it looks like each planet wanders across the sky against an unchanging background of stars.

Venus

Venus is the next planet out from the Sun. It is about the same size as **Earth** (it has a diameter of 12,100 km).

Venus has a very thick **atmosphere** and is completely covered by clouds. Sunlight reflecting off the **clouds** makes Venus look like a bright star when you see it in the sky. The clouds stop us seeing the surface of Venus, but **spacecraft** have been able to map the surface using **radar**.

This is a radar map of what Venus looks like under the blanket of cloud. It looks a bit like Earth with mountains and deep flat regions that look like seas.

Venus is extremely hot, nearly 500°C. There is no water on Venus so it would not be possible to live there.

Radar maps are made by bouncing radio waves off the surface of Venus. This measures the height of the surface. Then the map is coloured in by computer with blue for lowlands and pink for highlands.

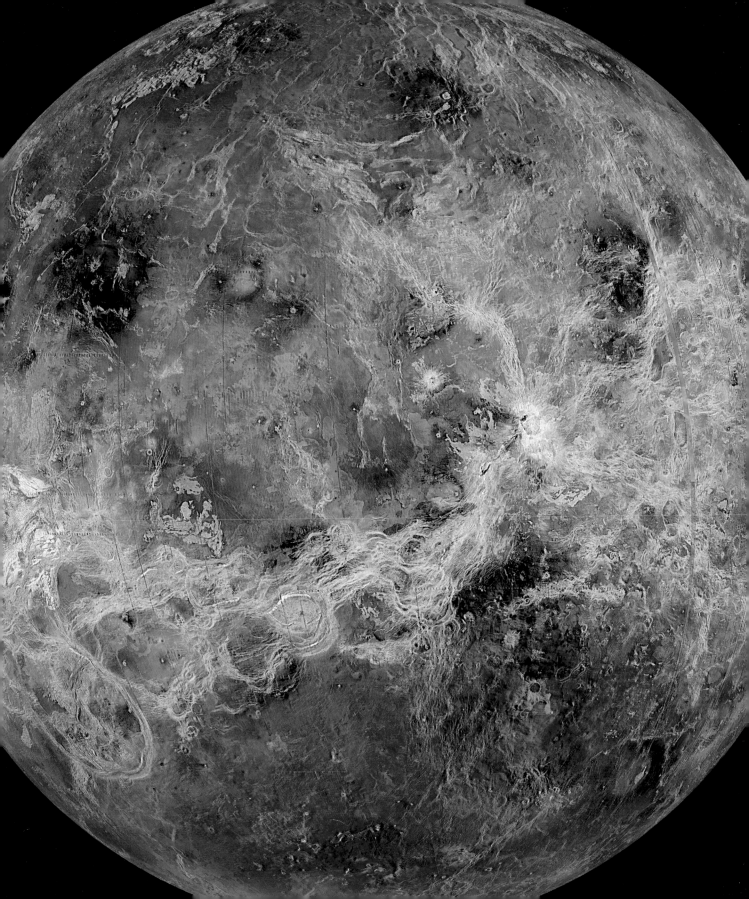

Earth

This is Earth, the planet we live on. It is the third planet out from the Sun. It has a diameter of 12,760 km.

Earth's atmosphere is not as thick and cloudy as Venus, which allows sunlight to reach the ground. Even on a very rainy day, when you might not think there is any sunshine, there is still a lot of light from the sun reaching the surface of Earth.

Earth is just the right temperature for liquid water to flow on its surface. This makes it possible for us to live on Earth.

In pictures taken from **space** our planet looks very blue. This is because so much of its surface is covered by oceans. Some people think that from space Earth looks like a blue marble.

Which continents can you identify in this picture? You should be able to pick out India and Africa.

The Life Zone

As far as we know, life can only exist on a planet where there is liquid water. Our word for a place where there is no water, 'desert', is the same as our word for a place where there is no life. The 'life zone' around a star is the region where it is too warm for water to freeze and too cool for water to boil.

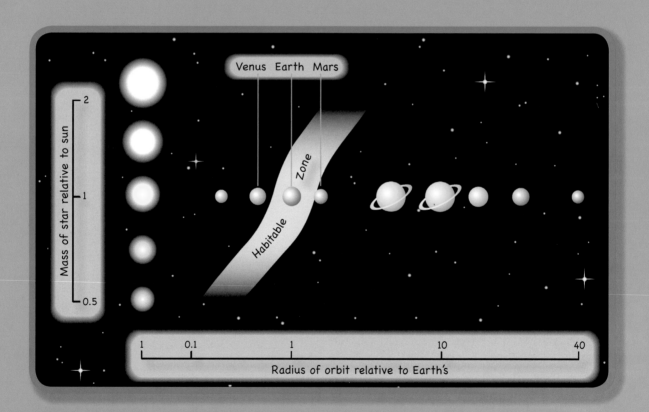

This diagram shows the extent of the life zone around different kinds of star. The Sun is in the middle, with the planets of the Solar System in order. Earth is in the middle of the life zone. Venus is just too close to the Sun for life, and Mars is just too far away. Smaller stars are cooler than the Sun, and bigger stars are hotter than the Sun. So for smaller stars, the life zone is closer to the star, whereas for larger stars it is farther away.

The size of a star in this diagram is measured in terms of its mass. Mass is like weight: if a star has half as much mass as the Sun, that means there is half as much stuff (matter) in it. Small stars are red and dim, big stars are blue-white and hot.

Mars

Mars is the next planet out from the Sun. It is only 6,800 km across, smaller than Earth but bigger than the Moon.

These pictures have been taken by a spacecraft orbiting the planet so you can see what Mars looks like if you could travel all around it.

Mars has a thin atmosphere, even thinner than the air on top of a very high mountain on Earth, but it is very dry with only a tiny amount of water. Like on Earth and on Venus there are mountains and lowlands, but Mars is too cold and dry and the air is too thin for any living thing to survive.

The Surface of Mars

Spacecraft have landed on Mars, but so far they have always been **unmanned**.

Phoenix is a spacecraft that sat on the surface of Mars for several months, sending back photographs and other information about the planet. After five months it ran out of power. It is still there, but cannot send back any more pictures.

This picture was taken by Phoenix in October 2008 and it shows the dry desert-like surface of Mars.

If you were on Mars you would have to wear a **spacesuit** as the atmosphere there is too thin for you to breathe.

Mars has the highest volcano in the Solar System. This Martian mountain is called Mount Olympus and it is more than 25 km tall, over three times higher than the tallest mountain on Earth, Mount Everest.

Jupiter

Jupiter is the largest planet in the Solar System. It is 143,000 km across and it is big enough to fit more than a thousand planets the size of Earth inside it.

This picture was taken from Earth using quite a small **telescope**, and shows Jupiter with just three of its many moons. The moons go round Jupiter just like planets going round the Sun, so it is as if Jupiter has a mini Solar System of its own.

Four hundred years ago, the Italian astronomer, **Galileo**, used one of the first telescopes to look at Jupiter and he saw almost exactly what we can see in this picture. Galileo showed that moons go around Jupiter and this convinced people that all the planets (including Earth) orbit the Sun.

Apart from the Moon and Venus, Jupiter is the brightest object in the night sky. So you should be able to see Jupiter quite clearly, and if you have some **binoculars** you might even be able to see some of its moons (as long as you keep the binoculars steady)!

Galileo Galilei was an Italian who lived four hundred years ago. He was one of the first people to use a telescope to look at the heavens, and he wrote a book called The Starry Messenger about his discoveries.

The Great Red Spot

Jupiter is just a huge ball of gas with no solid surface to land on beneath its clouds, but there might be a small solid core far below the clouds.

The stripy patterns in Jupiter's atmosphere are caused by winds going round the planet. In this picture you can see an area called the Great Red Spot, which is like an enormous whirling **hurricane** in the atmosphere of Jupiter. It is so vast that if you dropped the Earth on top of it our planet would just disappear. The winds in this hurricane have been blowing for at least four hundred years.

Just below Jupiter you can see one of its moons, which is called Ganymede.

Saturn

Saturn is one of the most beautiful and instantly recognisable planets. This is because it has a series of bright rings, as well as lots of moons going round it.

You can see the rings in this photograph, taken by a spaceprobe called Voyager that visited Saturn.

Lots of people assume that there is just one solid ring around Saturn, but that is not the case. There are lots of rings and they are each made up of tiny pieces of rock and ice that go round the planet like millions and millions of tiny moons.

The outermost ring whirling around Saturn is called the E ring and it is really huge (340,000 km in diameter).

The Voyager spacecraft took this close-up picture of Saturn's rings. The colouring has been added to the rings so that they can be seen more clearly. The millions of lumps of rock and ice in Saturn's rings form up into thousands of small ringlets. These ringlets whirl around together as part of the bigger rings surrounding Saturn.

Uranus

Uranus and Neptune are the farthest planets away from the Sun in our Solar System. They are made mostly of gas.

Did you know that Uranus also has a ring around it? It is not as easy to see as Saturn's rings. Uranus is orbited by seventeen small moons.

The temperature on Uranus is about -224°C. That is far colder than anywhere on Earth. The lowest temperature on Earth was recorded at Vostok base in Antarctica, where the temperature reached -89.2°C.

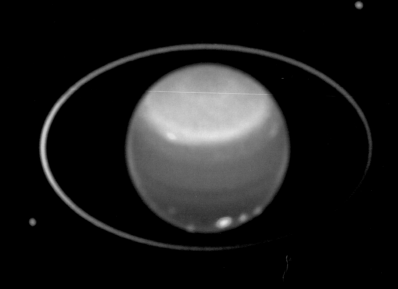

Neptune

Neptune is the farthest planet away from the Sun, so it is as cold as Uranus and very dark.

Neptune has been visited by one spacecraft, Voyager 2, which flew past on 25 August 1989.

Curiously, although modern **astronomers** only discovered Neptune in 1846, drawings made by Galileo nearly four hundred years ago show that he saw Neptune on 28 December 1612, and again on 27 January 1613. On both occasions, Galileo mistook Neptune for a star.

Large dark spots come and go in the atmosphere of Neptune, but they do not last as long as Jupiter's Great Red Spot.

Pluto

Pluto is known as a dwarf planet, because it is too small to be a proper planet. But people used to think it was a planet.

It is an icy lump only 2,400 km in diameter (smaller than our Moon) and orbits at the edge of the Solar System. There are many other dwarf planets in this part of space. Some people call them **plutoids**.

From Pluto, the Sun would just look like a bright star. No spaceprobe has yet reached Pluto. This picture was taken by the **Hubble Space Telescope**, which is in orbit around the Earth. It shows Pluto and one of its moons called Charon. It is the best view of Pluto we can get from Earth.

A spacecraft called New Horizons is on its way there. If all goes well it should reach Pluto in July 2015, and it will send back amazing pictures. So don't forget to put the date in your diary and look out for it in the news!

Ground based

Hubble Space Telescope

Pluto

Charon

Beyond our Solar System

Our Sun is not the only star with a family of planets.

Astronomers have found that there are more than three hundred other stars which each have at least one planet going round them. These are all relatively nearby (or at least, near for a star!), because it is very hard to identify planets going round stars that are far away. The planets found are mostly quite big, even bigger than Jupiter. This is partly because it is easier to find big planets than small planets.

Astronomers think that almost every star in the Milky Way has a family of planets. This means that there must be other planets like the Earth somewhere out there.

In March 2009, a satellite called Kepler was launched into orbit to look for other planets like Earth. It will spend more than three years studying 100,000 stars similar to our Sun with its telescopes. If it is successful, the next edition of this book will have to be a lot bigger!

Glossary

Astronomer
A scientist who studies the Universe of planets, stars and moons.

Atmosphere
The layer of gas surrounding a planet.

Binoculars
A pair of small telescopes joined together so both eyes can use them at once.

Clouds
A mass, as of dust, smoke, or water droplets, suspended in the atmosphere or in outer space.

Crater
The scar on the surface of a planet or moon made when it is hit by a lump of rock from space.

Diameter
The distance from one side to the other of a circle or a sphere.

Earth
Our home in space. A planet that goes round the Sun once every year.

Galileo Galilei
Italian astronomer who discovered the moons of Jupiter.

Hubble Space Telescope
A telescope flying in space, in orbit around the Earth. It is named after a famous astronomer, Edwin Hubble.

Hurricane
A very large storm with powerful winds sweeping around its centre.

Moon
With a capital 'M' for our Moon. With a small 'm', any object in orbit around a planet.

Orbit
The path followed by a planet as it goes round the Sun, or by a moon as it goes round a planet, or by a satellite like the Hubble Space Telescope as it goes round the Earth.

Planet
A cold lump of rock and gas that moves around a star in an orbit.

Plutoids
Icy lumps of rock at the edge of the Solar System, too small to be planets. Named after Pluto.

Radar
A way to measure distances to things by bouncing radio waves off them.

Radio waves
A kind of invisible light, like light waves but with much longer wavelengths.

Solar System
The Sun and its family of planets.

Space
The region beyond Earth's atmosphere.

Spacecraft
A vehicle for travelling into space.

Spaceprobe
Unmanned robot spacecraft sent to explore moons and planets.

Spacesuit
An airtight suit that astronauts wear so that they can breathe when they are somewhere where there is no air, like the surface of the Moon.

Star
A huge ball of hot gas, many times bigger than the Earth. It shines because it is hot.

Sun
The nearest star to us. The Sun is an ordinary star and only looks special because it is so close.

Telescope
An arrangement of lenses or mirrors (or both) that enables better views of distant objects.

Unmanned
Without people on board.

For Bella

The authors thank the Alfred C. Munger Foundation for support.

Photo credits

A. Pasten, A. Gomez and NOAO/AURA/NSF: 19; NASA: ESA: 2; Jet Propulsion Laboratory (JPL): 4, 24, 25; GRIN: 23; JPL/Cornell: 16,17; P. Jones, T. Clancy, S. Lee: 15; Johns Hopkins University Applied Physics Laboratory/ Carnegie Institution of Washington: 6; Tony Gray: 28; JPL/USGS: 9; Visible Earth (http://visibleearth.nasa.gov): 10. NASA/ E Karkoschka (Univ Arizona): 20. Tunc Tezel: 3

A CIP catalogue record for this book is available from the British Library.

First published in the UK in 2009 by the National Maritime Museum, Greenwich, London SE10 9NF
www.nmm.ac.uk/publishing

Text © John and Mary Gribbin

Hardback: 978-1-906367-17-6
Paperback: 978-1-906367-26-8

Printed in China